INVASIVE SPECIES
SNAKEHEAD FISH

by Emma Huddleston

FOCUS READERS.

NAVIGATOR

WWW.FOCUSREADERS.COM

Focus Readers is distributed by North Star Editions:
sales@northstareditions.com | 888-417-0195

Produced for Focus Readers by Red Line Editorial.

Content Consultant: Dr. Trevor J. Krabbenhoft, Assistant Professor of Biological Sciences, University at Buffalo

Photographs ©: USGS and USFWS/Science Source, cover, 1; Shutterstock Images, 4–5, 8–9, 12, 15, 19 (native fish), 19 (snakehead fish), 29; Buck Albert/USGS, 7; Red Line Editorial, 11; Alex Dorgan-Ross/AP Images, 16–17; iStockphoto, 19 (background, plants, insects, worm), 19 (fisher), 19 (frog); Paulo Oliveira/Alamy, 21; Ryan Hagerty/USFWS, 22–23, 27; Steve Ruark/AP Images, 25

Library of Congress Cataloging-in-Publication Data
Names: Huddleston, Emma, author.
Title: Snakehead fish / by Emma Huddleston.
Description: Lake Elmo, MN : Focus Readers, [2022] | Series: Invasive species | Includes index. | Audience: Grades 4-6
Identifiers: LCCN 2021003753 (print) | LCCN 2021003754 (ebook) | ISBN 9781644938584 (hardcover) | ISBN 9781644939048 (paperback) | ISBN 9781644939505 (ebook) | ISBN 9781644939918 (pdf)
Subjects: LCSH: Snakeheads (Fish)--Juvenile literature. | Introduced fishes--Juvenile literature. | Pest introduction--Juvenile literature. | Nature--Effect of human beings on--Juvenile literature.
Classification: LCC QL638.C486 H83 2022 (print) | LCC QL638.C486 (ebook) | DDC 597/.64--dc23
LC record available at https://lccn.loc.gov/2021003753
LC ebook record available at https://lccn.loc.gov/2021003754

Printed in the United States of America
Mankato, MN
082021

ABOUT THE AUTHOR

Emma Huddleston enjoys being a children's book author. When she's not writing, she can be found reading or running outside. She lives in Minnesota with her husband.

TABLE OF CONTENTS

CHAPTER 1

MONSTER FISH

A bluegill swims out of a patch of weeds. The small fish makes its way into a muddy area of the water. Suddenly, a snakehead fish snaps up the bluegill. The snakehead's pointy teeth make it a fierce hunter. However, this **invasive species** is having a harmful effect on certain areas.

The bluegill is a popular catch for fishers in the United States.

The snakehead is a large fish. It often weighs 10 to 12 pounds (4.5–5.4 kg). Its body can grow up to 5 feet (1.5 m) long. As a result, the snakehead is sometimes called a monster fish. It is causing problems in several areas of the United States.

For example, snakeheads live in the Potomac River. This freshwater river flows into the salty Chesapeake Bay. In fact, snakeheads have spread to many rivers that flow into the bay.

In 2012, people discovered snakehead fish in one of these rivers. Scientists studied the snakeheads' impact. They counted dozens of fish **species**. They

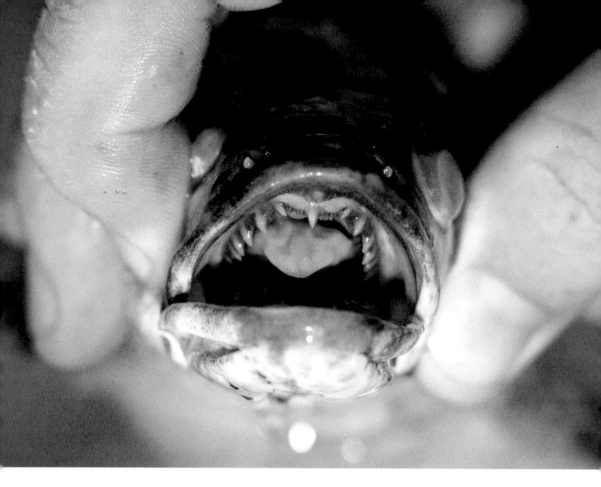

Some snakeheads are called Frankenfish due to their scary appearance.

learned that at least 17 of those species were smaller in number. Scientists also found many of those fish inside snakeheads' stomachs. Snakeheads were killing huge numbers of fish.

CHAPTER 2

SPREADING AROUND THE WORLD

Snakeheads are freshwater fish. Snakehead species can be divided into two main types. *Channa* species are native to Malaysia, India, and China. *Parachanna* are from **tropical** Africa.

In their native **habitats**, snakeheads live in rivers, streams, ponds, and lakes. They can handle a wide range of water

Scientists have discovered at least 29 species of snakehead.

temperatures. Snakeheads tend to live in places with lots of aquatic plants. They breed, feed, and build nests in the plants. Snakeheads have some predators in native areas. These predators keep snakehead **populations** down. As a result, native **food webs** remain balanced.

In the early 1900s, people brought snakeheads to Japan on purpose. People also brought them to the Philippines and Madagascar. The fish provided a new source of food for people. But over time, snakeheads spread to wild habitats.

People also spread the fish by mistake. They accidentally shipped snakeheads with bigheaded carp. Snakeheads spread to Central Asia. In the 1950s, they reached Russia and some Pacific islands.

People discovered snakeheads in the United States in 2002. That year, a fisher caught a snakehead in Maryland.

SNAKEHEAD RANGE IN THE UNITED STATES AS OF 2020

NORTHERN SNAKEHEAD   BULLSEYE SNAKEHEAD

As bullseye snakeheads get older, they often become darker in color.

A man from Maryland had bought live snakeheads in New York. He'd planned to cook them, but his sister didn't want to eat them. So, he released the fish into the wild. That started the spread.

As of 2020, the northern snakehead was the most widespread snakehead species. The fish were breeding in several US states. They were spreading in Arkansas and on the East Coast.

Bullseye snakeheads had also begun spreading in southern Florida. Snakeheads have spread in multiple ways. People release snakeheads into the wild. People also sell them in pet stores, restaurants, and live fish markets.

PRAYER RELEASE

Snakeheads are affected by some religious traditions. In these traditions, people buy animals from pet stores. Then they release the animals into the wild. This tradition is part of a prayer. The prayer shows one's kindness to a god. This practice has led to the spread of snakeheads in new areas.

SURVIVING ON LAND

Most fish cannot survive for long out of water. But snakeheads can. They can get oxygen from air and water. A snakehead has small pouches above its gills. These pouches fill up with air and let the fish breathe. A snakehead can survive on land for a few days. However, the fish will die if its body dries out.

A snakehead can also wiggle across land. To do so, it pushes its body with its tail. The large fins near its head keep the fish steady. Snakeheads sometimes do this to reach a new body of water. But they do not travel very fast or far.

In Madagascar, some snakeheads have a unique hunting method. First, the fish goes onto shore. Next, it lets its body become covered in

Snakeheads' ability to survive on land sets them apart from many other kinds of fish.

ants. Then, it returns to the water. The ants lose their grip and fall off the fish. Then the snakehead eats the ants.

CHAPTER 3

AGGRESSIVE PREDATOR

Not every **introduced species** is invasive. A species is invasive only if it changes native food webs. Snakeheads are invasive. That's partly because they can survive in many habitats. This ability helps them spread to new areas.

The fish can also breed quickly. Female snakeheads can carry up to 50,000 eggs.

Young snakehead fish are known as fry.

Not all of those eggs hatch. But mothers and fathers both guard the eggs after birth. They give their young a better chance to survive.

In addition, adult snakeheads face few predators in new places. Some birds, catfish, and larger fish feed on young snakehead fish. But once a snakehead grows larger than 5 pounds (2.3 kg), the fish becomes difficult for other animals to hunt. As a result, there are no animals to control snakehead populations.

When snakehead numbers are high enough, they can change native food webs. That's because the fish are aggressive predators. They threaten native species during all stages of their lives. Young snakeheads eat plants, bugs, tiny eggs, and small fish. Adults feed on other fish, frogs, small snakes, and lizards. Sometimes they even eat small

FRESHWATER FOOD WEB

Snakeheads lower populations of native fish. This takes away food sources from other animals.

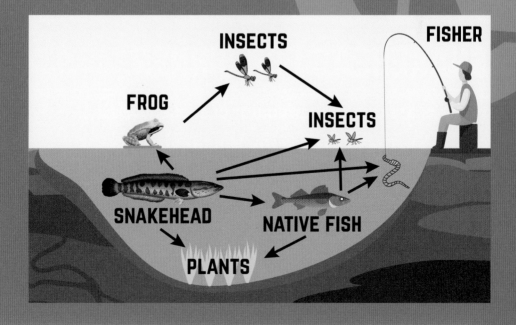

birds and **mammals**. Snakeheads lower the populations of other species. Some of those species could die off forever.

Snakeheads also compete with local animals for living space and food. Their large numbers force native species to move. That changes the balance of food sources. With less shelter and fewer food options, native animals may die off.

SNAKEHEAD FOR DINNER

Humans are one main predator of snakeheads. Farmers in China harvest the fish for food. One popular soup in China features snakehead. People cook snakehead in the United States, too. They grill, bake, and fry the fish. Many people compare its taste with that of whitefish.

A 2016 study found more than 21,000 snakeheads along a 120-mile (190-km) stretch of the Potomac River.

In the Potomac River, snakeheads eat most other fish. They have destroyed groups of shad, largemouth bass, and American eel. The American eel was already at risk. In Madagascar, snakeheads threaten cichlid fish. Some cichlids are found only in Madagascar. If they die off there, they will be **extinct**.

CHAPTER 4

CATCHING SNAKEHEADS

People are managing snakehead fish in many ways. In 2002, the US government banned bringing in snakehead fish from other countries. It also banned moving them from state to state without permission. States have taken action, too. Some have made owning snakeheads against the law.

A scientist measures a northern snakehead caught in Maryland waters.

These states include Alabama, California, Florida, and Texas. But laws do not stop everyone. Some people still bring in snakeheads from other countries.

Laws also cannot remove the fish already in the United States. So, some people catch snakeheads with nets. Others have tried draining lakes. Some people have even used poison. But all of these methods can harm native fish.

In 2009, officials in Arkansas did not want to take any chances. They decided getting rid of snakeheads was most important. Workers loaded helicopters with poison. Pilots dropped poison over waterways in Arkansas. The effort did not

In 2002, scientists sprayed poison in the Maryland pond where snakeheads were first found in the United States.

completely wipe out snakeheads in the area. But it may have stopped the fish's numbers from getting out of control.

People also tried poison in a Maryland pond. They dumped the poison into the water, and it killed all fish. They discovered six adult snakeheads and more than 1,000 young snakeheads had been living there. The poison worked, but it also harmed other wildlife.

In many areas, poison is not an option. Preventing the spread of snakeheads can work best. That's why scientists continue to study snakeheads. They teach people

ELECTROFISHING

Electrofishing is a type of fishing that uses electricity. Boats trail metal wires in the water. The wires are charged with electricity. If fish get too close to a wire, they can get shocked. The shock knocks fish out so they can be easily gathered up. But it doesn't kill them. So, sometimes fish get away. Fishers have used this type of fishing in the Potomac. They have caught hundreds of snakeheads.

Scientists use electrofishing to catch northern snakeheads.

about the fish, too. Government workers also partner with local fishers. Fishers report to the government where they caught snakeheads. That way, scientists can better track the fish's spread.

That information is important. It suggests where snakeheads may spread to next. People can work to keep the fish out of those places. Tracking helps even if snakeheads spread to new waters. People often notice the spread sooner. Government workers can also respond more quickly. And control methods work better when started sooner. Fish are easier to remove. They have less time to breed in large numbers.

People sometimes put on snakehead fishing contests. For instance, more than 100 people participated in the 2019 Maryland Snakehead Fishing Derby. Fishers caught 25 snakeheads in five hours. The largest weighed more than 10 pounds (4.5 kg). These kinds of events

Catching snakeheads can be a fun activity that also helps control their spread.

help limit snakehead numbers. They are also a way for more people to learn about snakeheads.

Snakehead fish have spread to many bodies of water. They harm wildlife and take over living spaces. They also disrupt food webs. However, many people are working to slow their spread and help native species.

FOCUS ON
SNAKEHEAD FISH

Write your answers on a separate piece of paper.

1. Write a sentence that describes the main ideas of Chapter 4.

2. Do you think it's worth removing an invasive species if native species would also be harmed? Why or why not?

3. How many eggs can an adult female snakehead carry at once?

     A. 10,000
     B. 25,000
     C. 50,000

4. How do invasive snakehead fish change native food webs?

     A. They kill native species and take food away from other native fish.
     B. They provide food for many natural predators.
     C. They disappear quickly and allow other fish to take over.

Answer key on page 32.

GLOSSARY

extinct
No longer living on Earth.

food webs
The feeding relationships among different living things.

habitats
The types of places where plants or animals normally grow or live.

introduced species
Plants or animals brought to an ecosystem by people instead of developing as part of the ecosystem.

invasive species
Plants and animals that people bring to a new place and that harm people, native plants, or native animals.

mammals
Animals that have hair and produce milk for their young.

populations
Groups of animals living in particular areas.

species
Groups of animals or plants that are alike and can breed with one another.

tropical
Having weather that is usually warm and wet.

TO LEARN MORE

BOOKS

Ciletti, Barbara J. *Northern Snakeheads*. Mankato, MN: Black Rabbit Books, 2017.

Gilles, Renae. *Invasive Species in Infographics*. Ann Arbor, MI: Cherry Lake Publishing, 2021.

Wilcox, Merrie-Ellen. *Nature Out of Balance: How Invasive Species Are Changing the Planet*. Custer, WA: Orca Book Publishers, 2021.

NOTE TO EDUCATORS

Visit **www.focusreaders.com** to find lesson plans, activities, links, and other resources related to this title.

INDEX

Answer Key: 1. Answers will vary; **2.** Answers will vary; **3.** C; **4.** A